OUTCOMPETE

How startups and billion-dollar companies outsmart the competition

MAYUR PALTA

ISBN: 9798392136193

PRAISE FOR OUTCOMPETE

"Mayur has deep understanding of "outcompeting" as he has lived it working at some of the leading corporations. This book is a must for any business leader!" ~ Farhat Ali, COO Sentry AI. Former President & CEO, Fujitsu America

"Outcompete introduces a new way to think about competition and how to buckle up for the uncertain times to come in the AI first world." ~ Rens ter Weijde, CEO KIMO

"In Outcompete", Mayur Palta answers the critical question of our times: "how can you compete in an AI world?" Learn from his experiences as an entrepreneur, technologist, and lifelong student while supporting education of underprivileged children with purchase of this book." ~ Anneke Seley, CEO Realty Works. Coauthor, Sales 2.0 & Next Era Selling

"Mayur has a great ability to grasp a vast array of technical, legal, financial, and business aspects. This book provides a clear system to follow for every business leader who wants to be at the helm and benefit from every tailwind available." ~ Otto Kekäläinen, Former CEO Maria DB Foundation

"Mayur Palta's 'Out Compete' masterfully deciphers the competitive business arena, rendering priceless strategies for startups and established businesses alike. This compelling read synthesizes his rich experiences, offering an unparalleled roadmap to outshine the competition." ~ George Molakal, CEO ALCOR Fund

"In technology business, either you are number 1 or number 0, it is indeed ruthless. Mayur, with his years of experience, brings lot of knowledge on how to outmaneuver the competition. I recommend this book for any aspiring Entrepreneur." ~ Sai Gundavelli, CEO Solix Technologies

"If innovation is on your agenda, this is a must read." ~PK Agarwal, Dean, University of California, Santa Cruz

MEET THE AUTHOR

Mayur Palta: With over 20 years of leadership and competitive strategy experience, Mayur's passion lies in teaching leaders and organizations how to outcompete the competition.

Mayur is a successful competitive strategist, entrepreneur, and technologist with a focus on helping fast-growing technology companies beat their competition.

A Harvard Business School Alumnus, Mayur is a recognized thought leader in competitive intelligence and strategy. Mayur popularized a novel competitive framework called The Outcompete Operating System (O2S) and introduced the world to seven new strategic principles for business leaders to win in times of uncertainty. Mayur's work uncovered the concept of a competitive intelligence flywheel.

Mayur's body of work in the field of competitive strategy spans 21 years of experience and hard-learned lessons from competitive failures, price wars, and successes in the fast-paced industries of technology, telecom, and chemical manufacturing.

Mayur held leadership roles at Fortune 500 companies like Oracle, Dell EMC, and Amazon as well as founded startups in telecom and chemical manufacturing. Mayur has been featured on various media platforms and podcasts.

Additionally, Mayur is a dedicated volunteer who supports nonprofits that provide education for underprivileged children.

To learn more about his work, visit www.mayurpalta.com

WHY THIS BOOK?

Lean towards the future, learn from the past, and do good!

1. **Lean towards the future:** Discover more ideas and strategies that you can apply to your career and your business. You'll collect actionable techniques you can use right away in your business. The hard fact of life is that people who read business books tend to earn more money.

2. **Learn from the past:** This book will offer you a different perspective and 'lessons learned' from real-life situations like failing a business, price wars, telecom wars, software wars, cloud wars, and now AI wars.

3. **Do good:** Proceeds from this book will go towards empowering underprivileged children with the gift of education.

Learn more at www.outcompetebook.com

WHY I WROTE THIS

DO YOU HAVE A GRIP ON YOUR COMPETITION OR DOES YOUR COMPETITION HAVE A GRIP ON YOU?

Most business leaders face similar competitive frustrations - losing business to competitors, declining market share, and being uninformed about frequent changes in the competitive landscape.

You're reading this book because you want to compete effectively and win. You already may have some wins under your belt, and now you're ready to win more. However, with this big challenge comes a new set of obstacles; what worked in the past may not work anymore. What got you here may not get you there.

What if I told you that by reading this book and applying its structured model and core principles, you could put all your competition-related frustrations to rest? That you could strengthen your organization's competitive muscle to creating lasting success?

Put this system to work and you will accomplish all the above, just as some of the billion-dollar companies and lean but mighty startups have been doing for years.

This book is based on real-world experiences, practical hard learned wisdom, and timeless truths. Most importantly, it works. Through hands-on experience, I have developed a practical but thorough method to help you outcompete and outsmart your top competitors.

If you're like most entrepreneurs or business leaders, you're probably experiencing one of the five common frustrations:

1. Losing business to competitors. You're frustrated about losing business to competitors and the revenue gap due to competitive losses is growing. Your competitors keep stealing your top customers. Your market share is declining.

2. Lack of awareness. You've no clue about which direction your top competitors are marching towards. It is becoming increasingly difficult to make sense of the rapidly changing competitive landscape.

3. Lack of organizational readiness. You're frustrated with your teams like field sales, product, marketing, and partners. They don't seem to understand your competitive differentiation and are always seeking discounts to undercut the competition, negatively eroding your profit margins.

4. Revenue stagnation. Your revenue growth has stalled. You're concerned either the market is slowing down, or you are losing to competitors that you don't even know yet. You feel overwhelmed and unsure of what to do next.

5. Nothing's working. You've tried several things with strategic initiatives and competitive readiness efforts. None worked and the efforts had no material impact on your ability to compete effectively and win.

Overall, you have been experiencing this pain for some time now, you tried to do something about it, and it didn't work. The elephant in the room is,

"Are you committed to fixing it NOW?

"And what are you going to do about it?

Well, good news: we have some answers!

The Outcompete Operating System (O2S) is a practical method for achieving competitive advantage you have always envisioned.

In this book, you'll learn the secrets of strengthening the four key components of your competitive strategy. You'll discover a simple yet powerful way to outsmart the competition that will give you and your leadership team more confidence, higher win rates, and more peace of mind. Successful companies are applying Outcompete every day to run profitable and frustration-free businesses in hypercompetitive industries- and you can too.

I wrote this book with two specific categories of audiences in mind:

1. Founders in High Technology and related industries interested in getting a grip on their competition. Whether you live in Silicon Valley or are operating your venture from anywhere around the world, you can appreciate the aggressive nature of the competition in the fast-paced technology world. Perhaps, you subscribe to the long-held belief that software is eating the world or the newly evolving belief that artificial intelligence will eat all of software. This book will help you shape how you think about competition and offer a ready to deploy operating system that you can leverage to outcompete the competition.

2. Business Leaders Operating in Hypercompetitive Markets. Whether you are a Chief Executive Officer (CEO), Chief Revenue Officer (CRO), Chief Marketing Officer (CMO), Chief Product Officer (CPO), Sales Strategy leader, or Head of Competitive Intelligence (CI)/Strategy, we all face competitive obstacles in our own unique way.

> As a CEO, you're frustrated with the lack of a cohesive competitive strategy that is neither effective nor scalable. Your business is losing market share to competitors, the revenue growth is slowing down, and board wants to know what you are going to do about it. You're on the hook to keep a close eye on the changing market landscape, monitor the trends, and identify market opportunities to leapfrog the competition.
>
> As a CRO, you're concerned about missing your revenue goals because of losing deals to competitors. Instead of losing to 'do nothing', you're losing to competitors. You're trying to get a handle on why customers are choosing your competitors over you and neither your sales leaders nor CRM (Customer Relationship Management) systems are offering any meaningful or rational answers.
>
> As a CMO, you're struggling to land your key differentiators with prospects. Industry is moving towards commoditization and your existing competitive messaging isn't differentiated enough.
>
> As a CPO, your product or service has lost its competitive edge and competitors are iterating at a much faster pace of innovation than your product or service is. You're building your product based on an

obsolete technology or platform while your newly emerged competitor is a late entrant and is leveraging the cutting-edge technologies rendering your first mover advantage ineffective.

As a Sales Strategy Leader, you're frustrated with the lack of confidence in the field to take on competitors. You doubled the budget for competitive enablement but still it's not yielding the desired sales results.

As a Head of Competitive Intelligence (CI), you're unable to scale your efforts or team to match the growing scale of the business. You're working tirelessly to deliver competitive insights to the executives, but leaders are losing confidence in your ability to deliver timely and actionable insights. Your top competitors are bridging up the competitive gap.

Now, let's begin this journey by envisioning what your business could look like after implementing The Outcompete Operating System (O2S). The book is organized into three different parts: **Knowing, Doing, Being**

- Knowing the Outcompete Operating System model and lessons learned from technology rivalries
- Doing is about applying the strategic principles like building flywheels and communities, creating categories, and shaping the narrative
- Being a competitive strategist

THE OUTCOMPETE TOOLKIT

Want even better results and more business success?

Equip every person on your team with the right information and tools to run your company on The Outcompete Operating System (O2S). With the Outcompete Toolkit, everyone in the company - from leadership to functional leaders to competitive intelligence professionals - will understand their role and be empowered to help your company win against the competition.

Scan QR code below for Udemy Course:
Become Great at Beating the Competition

DEDICATION

To my dad, Ashok Chander Palta, one of the world's greatest entrepreneurs.
To my mom, Anjumn Palta, one of the world's most self-less human being.
This book would not exist without your teaching of life lessons. It is a tribute to who you both are.
To my sisters, brother and sister in laws, niece, and nephews.

And my wife, Isha, my sons, Ray and Aarin. I am so proud, and I love each of you with all my heart.

OUTCOMPETE

CONTENTS

PART I

KNOWING

Knowing the Outcompete Operating System model and lessons learned from technology rivalries.

THE

OUTCOMPETE

OPERATING SYSTEM

(O2S)

Outcompete Operating System (O_2S)

Oxygen for your Competitive Strategy

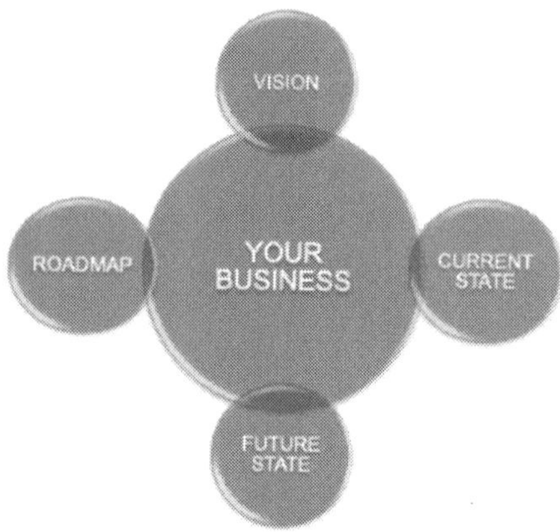

Learn more: outcompetebook.com

Every great system is made up of a grouping of core components. The same applies to a business. The Outcompete Operating System (O2S) identifies Four Key Components of any organization. You no longer must worry about dozens of different aspects of your competitive strategy. O2S is an operating system for gaining lasting competitive advantage.

In the words of an O2S client, *"I used to get overwhelmed with the ever-changing competitive landscape. It was very difficult to think clearly and simply about how our business can achieve lasting success. Now, I refer to O2S as the Oxygen (O2) for our Strategy."*

With O2S, the whole is greater than the sum of its parts. It's a powerful tool for identifying your business's blind spots when it comes to competition.

Below are the Four Key Components of The Outcompete Operating System namely Competitive Vision aka Vision, Current State, Future State, and Roadmap.

Think of these as the "why", the "what, and the "how".

1. Vision is the why.
2. The current and future states are what.
3. The roadmap is the how.
4. The seven principles guide the roadmap, the how.

To apply O2S to your own business, you start with the why, then the what, and finally the how.

Let's discuss these four components.

VISION

Vision component focuses on the "why". Vision is the long-term competitive direction for your business. In this book, we will refer to competitive vision as vision given the topic at hand.

Think of the different visions that some of the largest brands in the world have made abundantly clear. E.g., Apple, which is the most valuable brand and has crossed $3 Trillion in market capitalization a few times, articulates its vision as "to make the best products on earth and to leave the world better than we found it." Apple's competitive vision is to be a data and AI company where data drives innovation at the intersection of software, hardware, and services.

To realize its competitive vision, Apple has tightly integrated its software, hardware, and services where the boundaries between the three are difficult to tell. In executing this competitive vision, Apple must provide prescriptive guidance to the whole company on, "tightly integrating data and AI at the intersection of software, hardware, and services while building products and services". Also, on "how to use Data and AI to their advantage in the next 3 to 5 years?".

Competitive vision tends to be fully aligned with the overall corporate. For example, Apple's competitive vision is tightly aligned to the overall corporate vision to make the best products, protect its brand, and create new sources of competitive advantage.

Answering the Questions

The first tool in O2S is the Vision (Competitive Vision). Not only is the Vision designed to get your vision out of your head and onto paper, but it will also help you answer these questions.

- Where do you see your business going in the next 3 to 5 years from a competitive standpoint?
- What specific position in your industry landscape are you aiming for?
- Do you want to gain market share based on cost leadership or differentiation?
- Do you aspire to be the leader in the industry defining the direction the entire industry is going?
- Do you anticipate market consolidation and your business to be on an acquisition spree? Or are you looking for a fruitful exit?

CURRENT STATE

Current state component focuses on the "what" - where you are today. Assessing your current competitive state is like reading the context as a new business leader coming into an organization to turn things around.

In Bill George and Zach Clayton's recent book 'True North', the authors surveyed its advisory council on the leader's most important quality, their answer was unanimous: self-awareness.

Know Thyself - Inscribed on temple wall at Delphi during 6th century BC.

Self-awareness is the foundation of authenticity. You develop it by exploring your life story and your crucible. Similarly, developing an objective and honest self-awareness of your business and its' current state is of paramount importance in shaping its future. For example, when Satya Nadella took over as Microsoft CEO from Steve Ballmer in 2014, Satya took the time to do an objective assessment of the current state of the business. Many business leaders refer to it as "reading the context".

In Microsoft's case, the company was suffering from a dysfunctional, political culture that had missed every significant technology innovation wave in the past decade, including internet search (to Google), mobile phones (to Apple among others), social media (to Facebook among others, and the cloud (to Amazon).

The current state component is an assessment of your business on multiple parameters like maturity of competitive intelligence function, accuracy in predicting/anticipating competitor's moves, field sales competitive confidence levels, and reliability of win loss data in CRM.

Answering the Questions

Here are a series of self-assessment questions business leaders must ask to baseline the current state:

- How mature are your business functions to react to competitive pressures? How closely and accurately are you able to anticipate competitive moves or product announcements?
- On a scale of 1 to 10 (1 - least mature to 10 - most mature), would you rate your competitive intelligence function?
- How confident does your field sales team feel about beating the top competitors?
- What are the current competitive win rates against the top three competitors?
- How accurate is the win loss data in your company's CRM (Customer Relationship Management) system like Salesforce?

FUTURE STATE

Future state component focuses on the "what" - where you want your business to be in the future. It is the north star of your business.

Continuing our example from the previous component, Satya Nadella painted a picture of the future for Microsoft where Microsoft is riding the technology innovation waves sooner, not missing them.

Upon taking the helm, Satya rapidly transformed Microsoft's strategy and culture, exiting its failed acquisition of Nokia mobile phones (yielding to Apple and Google), entering social media with the acquisition of LinkedIn (stealing LinkedIn under the nose of Marc Benioff and Salesforce), expanding its cloud business Azure (doubling down the investments, partnerships, and reach), and broadening into games with Minecraft regaining popularity) and Activision Blizzard. Under Ballmer, Microsoft's stock had been flat for about 14 years.

Since Satya became CEO, Microsoft stock has grown nine times to a valuation of close to $2.5 trillion, making Microsoft one of the world's two most valuable companies. This story of continued renewal and hitting refresh on the future state continues with Microsoft's big bet on Generative AI and LLM (Large Language Models) with the $10 billion timely investment in OpenAI, putting Microsoft in the driver's seat shaping the future of Artificial Intelligence.

Answering the Questions

Here are a few self-assessment questions business leaders must ask to bring clarity about the future state:

- What specific strengths would you like the different business functions to develop to compete effectively?
- Will there be mechanisms or automation in place to be able to predict competitors' moves more proactively and accurately?
- How will you analyze the downstream impact of your competitors' moves like new product launches, acquisitions, or sales campaigns against you?
- What types of actionable insights would you like to see from mining your win loss data from your CRM (Customer Relationship Management) system(s)?

- How much reduction in effort do you expect from field sales in replicating lighthouse competitive wins?
- What aspirations do you have in improving your win rates against top competitors?

ROADMAP

Roadmap component focuses on the "how". Think of Roadmap as the established path to get your business from current state to future state on its competitive journey.

Take for example Amazon. For the longest time, lots of questions have been raised about the lack of Amazon's profitability as a business. Along the journey comes Amazon's massive cloud investments in AWS (Amazon Web Services), making Amazon profitable since 2014. To build its roadmap and execute, Amazon famously leverages its leadership principles and peculiar mechanisms. These principles guide the roadmap and how decisions are made.

Answering the Questions

Here are a few self-assessment questions business leaders must ask to build their roadmap:

- What specific set of actions will you take to realize your competitive vision?
- How will you move the needle from current state to future state?
- How will you bring about cultural, system, process, and people change to make progress towards the future state?
- How will change be managed to be least disruptive to the ongoing revenue streams?
- How will you explore new ways of beating the competition while exploiting your current tried and tested strengths in beating the competition?

Now you have a good understanding of The Outcompete Operating System model and its four key components.

In subsequent chapters, we will discuss seven strategic principles backed by stories from author's real-world experiences. These seven principles and lessons learned from these stories talk about "the how" of competitive strategy in today's uncertain times.

PART II

DOING

Doing is about applying the strategic principles like building flywheels and communities, creating categories, and shaping the narrative.

PRINCIPLE ONE

BUY YOUR WAY IN

MERGERS & ACQUISITIONS

In June 2010 on a hot summer late afternoon in Redwood Shores, California, I was about to wrap up my workday at Oracle's headquarters. At the time, I was in the field engineering organization at Oracle. I was leading a virtual team focused on competing for database software and had been at Oracle for about 5 years. I received a call from a coworker who seemed rushed and breathless. *"We got a dinner to go to, Mayur."*

I said, *"Are you sure? There is no such dinner scheduled on my calendar."*

She said, *"The CIO of one of our top customers agreed to meet with us for dinner. He is in town just for a day. This is our one shot. And I need you there."*

Two hours later, we were at a fine dining restaurant in San Jose, California. The CIO of this customer showed up all dressed up and before even sitting down said, *"Hello Oracle team, I cancelled my dinner plans with IBM and Microsoft to meet with you guys. Oracle has literally bought its way into my office. Now my CFO tells me Oracle is the top line item in our IT budget. So, I am here."*

Let's dive into how large billion-dollar corporations like Oracle and Dell go on an acquisition spree.

Oracle's Acquisition Spree

Between the years 2005 to 2016, I had the opportunity to work at Oracle Corporation. Oracle is one of the best places you can work at if you want to learn how to play to your strengths, compete effectively, and win. Afterall, Oracle was founded and is run by one of the most competitive men in the technology world, Larry Ellison. From battles of the technology titans over the last 40+ years to winning America's Cup, the Super Bowl of sailing, Larry wants to just win. As a result, the core DNA of Oracle and its employees is competitive. In fact, a strengths finder study at Oracle in the year 2012 confirmed so.

Oracle Corporation is an American multinational computer technology corporation headquartered in Austin, Texas. In 2020, Oracle was the third-largest software company in the world by revenue and market capitalization. The company sells database software and technology, cloud-engineered systems, and enterprise software products.

The flagship product for Oracle has been database software. Microsoft's CEO, Satya Nadella, was once asked what piece of technology you wish you owned at Microsoft. He said, "The Oracle Database".

In the 1970s, Larry Ellison, while routinely scanning the IBM Journal of Research and Development, discovered a research paper that described a working prototype for a relational database management system (RDBMS). Over the 1950s and 1960s, IBM's dominance of the computer market was almost complete, with the company making 60% to 70% of all business computers worldwide. Between 1975 and 1988, IBM mainframes slipped from 78 to 35 percent of U.S. computer sales.

During the 1980s and 1990s, IBM pioneered desktop computing and lost its status as the market leader. Clones of the IBM machine and business model quickly sprang up throughout the consumer market, with numerous other companies selling PC machines running Microsoft's operating system.

Oracle back in the day in 1977 started with the CIA as its first customer to offer database software. Oracle back in 1978 offered CIA version 2 of the Oracle database because Larry knew that no one adopts version 1 of any software. During the 1980s, full-scale war started between Oracle and IBM vying for market share for databases. It was almost like David (Oracle) taking on Goliath (IBM).

Competitive landscape

Database software wars have been one of the most heated and public wars between competitors since the 1990s. These competitive rivalries were so fierce and cutthroat that these are still remembered, studied, and taken inspiration from even today in 2023. During the 1990s, the four database players that competed most fiercely were Oracle, IBM, Informix, and Sybase. The big four – Oracle, IBM, Informix, and Sybase – lived and died by the Transaction Processing Council's (TPC-C) benchmarks, which simulated a computing environment where a population of users execute order-entry transactions against a database. One week, Oracle was #1 in the TPC-C benchmark, the next week, it was Sybase. And so on.

Around the year 2000, Oracle competed primarily in two layers of the technology stack namely, enterprise back-office applications and database software. The prime competitors for back-office applications included the likes of SAP, PeopleSoft, and JD Edwards. While the prime competitors for database software were mainly Microsoft SQL Server, IBM DB2, and Sybase. Over the next ten years, Oracle competed in multiple layers of the technology stack including Enterprise Applications, Middleware, Databases, Hardware, and Industry Applications.

One of Oracle's key strategies for market consolidation was to acquire smaller software companies that had complementary products or technologies. By acquiring these companies, Oracle was able to expand its product portfolio and market share, while also eliminating potential competition. Between the year 2003 and 2023, Oracle made close to 144 acquisitions spending $150 billion. Some of the famous acquisitions were the hostile takeover of PeopleSoft, stealing Sun Microsystems under the nose of IBM acquiring key intellectual property like Java, Solaris, and MySQL, and electronic medical record provider, Cerner.

Another important strategy was to form partnerships with other technology companies and industry leaders. These partnerships helped Oracle to develop new products and technologies, while also increasing its visibility and reputation in the industry.

Through these strategies, Oracle was able to consolidate the market and become one of the largest and most influential companies in the technology industry. Today, Oracle continues to innovate and expand its offerings, while also seeking out new partnerships and acquisitions to maintain its competitive edge.

Another "mega merger" I had the opportunity to experience is Dell and EMC.

Mega Merger: Dell EMC

On September 29th, 2016, I joined Dell EMC as an Enterprise System Engineering Manager. I was staring through the front glass of my car sitting in traffic on Highway 237, in the heart of Silicon Valley. Today was my first day at work at computer manufacturer Dell's newly merged company EMC forming Dell Technologies.

Previously, I had spent the last 11 years at Oracle, a predominantly software-focused corporation, living through multiple phases of digital disruption – converged infrastructure, big data, and cloud computing. I knew that the technology industry was getting disrupted by alternative business models like cloud computing from Amazon Web Services and the market was adjusting to the new rules of the game.

To make a meaningful impact in my new role, I would have to quickly read the broader context of the Dell EMC merger, anticipate the potential changes in the internal and external environment, and establish a course of action for future success in his district.

EMC Corporation

EMC Corporation is an American multinational corporation headquartered in Hopkinton, Massachusetts, United States. EMC sold data storage, information security, virtualization, analytics, cloud computing and other products and services that enabled businesses to store, manage, protect, and analyze data. EMC's target markets included large companies and small- and medium-sized businesses across various vertical markets. EMC had over 70,000 employees and was the world's largest provider of data storage systems by market share.

Merger

On October 12, 2015, Dell Inc. announced that it would acquire EMC in a cash-and-stock deal valued at $67 billion—the largest-ever acquisition in the technology industry. On July 19, 2016, EMC shareholders approved the merger agreement among Denali Holding Inc., Dell Inc., Universal Acquisition Co., and EMC. The merger transaction closed on September 7, 2016, and EMC's common shares were delisted from the New York Stock Exchange.

The merger closed on September 7, 2016. EMC had been renamed to Dell EMC and because of the merger, both Dell and EMC were now private companies forming Dell Technologies. Dell Technologies CEO Michael Dell explained that the purchase was meant to "evolve the company into the most relevant areas where IT is moving", combining Dell's enterprise server, personal computer, and mobile businesses with EMC's enterprise storage business.

A Tale of Two Distinct Business Models

EMC Federation

EMC Corp. (EMC) grew through acquisitions and operated a unique "federated business model". EMC had been a federation of six independently run businesses that operated as one giant company called the EMC Federation. The idea to cooperate — like creating a unified sales staff — to make each member stronger.

With EMC, VMware, RSA, and Pivotal as the four brands that made up the EMC federation, the businesses remained interdependent but still connected. That allowed EMC to provide customers with choices.

EMC Corporation excelled in winning and growing the customer share of wallet among large enterprise businesses and focused on technology differentiation to achieve high margins. As a result of this focus on the enterprise segment of the customer base, EMC went to market with a sizable field sales force and relied somewhat on channel partners to distribute to smaller businesses.

The high margins from large enterprise customers demanded an operating model focused around generating business value for customers and building long-term trusted relationships. Hence, the culture was employee friendly with benefits, perks, and rewarding tenure. Some in the sales function described the culture as "hero" culture wherein individual heroic contribution was recognized over a collective team effort.

Direct from Dell

From a dorm room at the University of Texas to the world's leading direct computer systems company, the story of Dell Computer Corporation reflected the pioneering vision of Michael Dell. Dell based his strategy on obtaining high growth with integrity and achieving market share the old-fashioned way: one customer at a time. By selling customized products directly to end customers, Dell had empowered businesses and consumers to choose the best solutions for their computing needs.

Dell Computer's principles of success: sell direct, keep inventory small, keep quality high and please your customers.

Dell excelled in maintaining direct customer sales and support channels, just-in-time inventory, and strong supply chain processes. Hence, the business model focused on large volumes with laser-thin margins and catered to businesses of all sizes, predominantly end consumers as well as small and medium businesses.

To cater to the demands of many customers globally, Dell went to market with a sizable inside sales team for a large volume of smaller businesses and offshore direct contact center-based sales and support for end consumers. The laser-thin margins and a large volume of orders demanded an operating model focused on metrics, efficiency, and strong cost controls. Hence, the culture focused on measuring efficiencies in the processes and metrics-based incentives.

Dell Technologies: Go Big! Win Big!

On September 7' 2016, Dell Technologies was formed as the largest private technology company in the world employing 140,000 employees including 40,000+ sales professionals, 30,000+ customer service and support professionals. With combined revenue of $74 Billion, Dell Technologies organized around three major business segments namely, Dell (the Client Solutions Group), Dell EMC (the Infrastructure Solutions Group); and the strategically aligned businesses: VMware, SecureWorks and Pivotal.

Infrastructure Solutions Group targeted 3,000 or so large enterprise customers under the leadership of legacy EMC leaders with a revenue goal of $18 Billion while Client Solutions Group targeted 500,000+ small and medium customers under the leadership of legacy Dell leaders with a revenue goal of $40 Billion. Rest of the customers globally were to be serviced by the indirect channel partners and distributors.

Competitive Landscape

The enterprise storage market was changing at a rapid pace. New technology inflection points such as flash-based arrays and software-defined storage had emerged to address the changing needs of today's data-intensive workloads. In addition, public cloud-based storage offerings from vendors like Amazon Web Services, Microsoft, and Google continued to make a permanent impact on enterprise storage economics and consumption models.

Big market shifts like these posed serious threats to the incumbent enterprise storage providers like Dell EMC, NetApp, Hewlett Packard Enterprise, and IBM who must innovate quickly to keep up. These vendors responded with new products and services to keep their businesses on track and remain relevant with both existing and new customers.

In the traditional enterprise storage world, Dell EMC products faced competition from NetApp, Hitachi Data Systems, Hewlett-Packard Company, IBM Corporation and Sun Microsystems. Furthermore, it also faced occasional competition from smaller niche players, such as Nutanix, PureLogic, and Violin Memory among several others.

NetApp

NetApp served customers in the energy, federal government, financial services, life sciences, manufacturing, telecommunications, high technology, and Internet industries. High technology start-ups grew at a frenetic pace, which also propelled NetApp to become a 2,200-employee-strong organization and generate over $1.1 billion in revenues by the fiscal year ending on April 30, 2001.

Ninety-two percent of its revenues came from the sale of its appliance products; the rest was split between professional services and software sales. NetApp had struggled over the last several years to keep pace with market change. For example, the company was late to the all-flash array party, missing much of the initial wave of testing and acceptance by early adopters.

In February 2016, the company announced a transformation initiative to get back on track with a focus on growth in new technologies along with a cost structure realignment. The latest effort as a part of this transformation was a 6% workforce reduction, announced in October 2016.

Hewlett Packard Enterprise

Michael Dell was betting big on scale and a model that he argued can be nimble. HPE CEO Meg Whitman believed you can't have it all so focus on speed and innovation. The two sides were duking it out in the data center world.

There may be no better technology business model for Petri dish than Hewlett Packard Enterprise vs. Dell Technologies in the years to come. Dell Technologies had been betting on scale, girth and hopes that a massive company can be nimble. HPE was focused on shedding units as fast as it can so it can focus on the hybrid cloud, software-defined infrastructure and move faster than larger rivals.

In 2015, Hewlett-Packard (before the HP and HP Enterprise split) was a soup-to-nuts IT vendor. PCs, printers, servers, networking, storage, and services were all under one roof. CEO Meg Whitman engineered a split in the name of focus. Hewlett-Packard became HP Enterprise and HP Inc., which had the PC and printing divisions. The sheer breadth of HPE's deconstruction was laid out in a slide. HPE spin-merges its enterprise services division to CSC for $8.5 billion and a similar transaction with Micro Focus for its software business worth $8.8 billion.

Amazon Web Services

EMC, like every other IT incumbent, had one nervous eye on Amazon Web Services, the public cloud giant that became a huge success largely because software developers saw it as a cheap, easy way to get the resources they need to build and test their products.

Amazon Web Services (AWS), a subsidiary of Amazon.com, offered a suite of cloud-computing services that make up an on-demand computing platform. AWS offered numerous storage services on a subscription pay-per-use basis which directly competed with Dell EMC's storage products. Over the last 10 years, AWS had grown to be a $10 Billion annual run rate business with a market cap of 10x revenue.

Overall, what we can learn from this mega merger of Dell EMC is that 'buying your way in' to consolidate the market in your favor can be an effective strategy if you have the money muscle to do so.

PRINCIPLE TWO

SCALE EFFECTIVELY

BUILD FLYWHEELS

The Competitive Intelligence Flywheel

Why do data-driven companies build competitive intelligence flywheels?

Data-driven companies can exploit market trends by creating reinforcing competitive intelligence feedback loops that give them competitive advantage over time. To predict the future, data-driven companies leverage their strengths like access to competitive data, access to the right data platforms, and access to data talent.

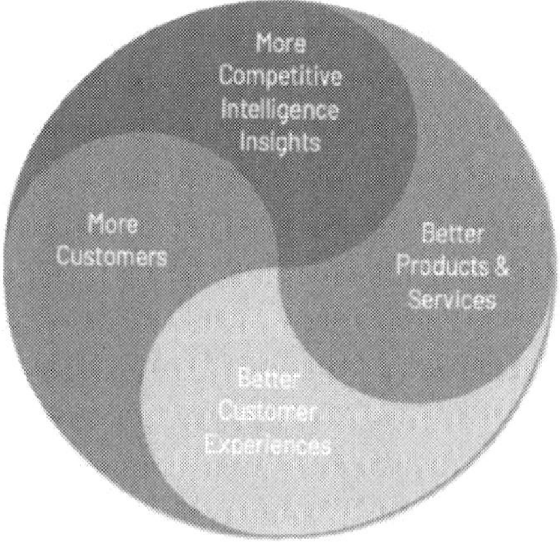

Consider the power of competitive data network effects. The more competitive insights one has, the better one can deliver on products/services; the better one can offer in terms of customer experiences, the more customers are attracted; the more customers one has, the more competitive insights one gets. This type of competitive intelligence flywheel makes a company attractive to customers and strengthens the company's ability to compete effectively, as the flywheel gains momentum.

Scan to read more: Building a competitive intelligence flywheel using data and artificial intelligence.

Let's dive deeper into one of the real-world competitive intelligence flywheels I had the opportunity to experience first-hand.

Cloud Wars: Amazon Web Services

On March 13th, 2017, I started at Amazon Web Services as a leader for one of the Solution Architecture teams in North America. A week into my role, I attended a training mandatory for managers focused on making great hiring decisions. The calendar invite for this training did not reveal the location of this in-person training. The night before this training, the location was added.

As I arrived at this location Monday morning, I realized that this place did not look like any of the typical Silicon Valley technology company offices. Few of my coworkers and I went through exceptionally high level of security checks before we were allowed in the building. The directions were no cellphones out of your pockets and no clicking of pictures. It turned out to be one of the AWS data centers. The training was taught by the leader managing that regional data center and we had once in a lifetime opportunity to be inside an AWS data center.

Driving back from this training, I started to think through the state of the cloud computing industry and what's ahead during this 25 minute or so drive.

State of AWS and cloud computing in early 2017

At the time, AWS grew 55% in the trailing 12 months resulting in $13+ billion in annual recurring revenue and was considered the fastest-growing multi-billion-dollar technology startup. While well-established technology companies like Oracle and IBM were growing in low single digits or declining, AWS was doubling in size every 2 to 3 years.

I started my career building my own businesses and at the time of joining AWS, had spent the prior 14 years in the technology industry at large well-established companies like Hewlett Packard, Oracle, and Dell EMC. Amazon's unique, strong, and peculiar culture was going to be an amazing cultural ride for me as I ramp up in my new role as a leader of the solutions architecture team at AWS in the western region of the Americas.

I was tasked with doubling the size of my team in a matter of few months while the AWS Solution Architect hiring process was hauntingly slow, the probability of a potential candidate clearing the interview process to an offer stage was 1 in 200 candidates that apply, and these challenges were even more amplified in a talent war area like Silicon Valley where top global technology brands like Apple, Google, Facebook, Netflix and hundreds of startups with a dream to be a unicorn one day were willing to burn any amount of cash and stock options to hire the top engineering talent in the world.

During that fiscal year, AWS was growing at the rate of 45%+ YoY and there were 5,600+ open roles to fill globally so everyone was hiring and, in some cases, competing for the same limited pool of talent. Because of the enormous possibilities within AWS and Amazon, there was tremendous mobility to move across roles, functions, departments, and even businesses within Amazon.

As a result, there was enormous competition internally to hire and develop the best. In my team, one of the Solution Architects transferred out to take another role within product at AWS putting even more pressure on the resources of the team to satisfy this accelerating pace of growth.

Amazon Web Services

Amazon.com, the parent company of AWS, decided around the year 2005 to refactor and decouple the infrastructure from the application so that new features could be rolled out easily. Also, so that the technology infrastructure could scale better and offer elasticity to meet the seasonal nature of Amazon.com's business.

Think of Amazon as a collection of startups where individuals internally can pitch to Jeff and form 2 pizza teams (a team that can be fed with 2 pizzas) to go live with AWS without doing the heavy lifting of infrastructure, servers, and databases. AWS was one such 2 pizza teams initially. While initially the objective was to cater to the internal demands of Amazon.com's technology infrastructure, eventually AWS was exposed to customers so that customers could leverage AWS to innovate at a faster pace. This way, a cost center like technology infrastructure could over time become a profit center.

Amazon Web Services (AWS), a subsidiary of Amazon.com offered a suite of cloud computing services that made up an on-demand computing platform. These services operated from 16 geographical regions across the world. Officially launched in 2006, Amazon Web Services initially provided online services for other websites or client-side applications. Swipe your credit card on a website and you have a server ready to use at the cost of a Starbucks coffee. The shadow IT groups for enterprises bypassed their internal IT teams and red tape to go straight to AWS for their computing needs. Startups no longer had to raise millions to buy Sun servers and Oracle database to get started anymore. AWS became the platform for builders and cloud computing changed the IT industry forever.

In June 2007, Amazon claimed that more than 180,000 developers had signed up to use Amazon Web Services. In November 2010, it was reported that all Amazon.com retail web services had been moved to AWS. This was a massive proof point for the naysayers who kept saying that cloud may not be a scalable and reliable solution to their computing needs.

In April 2015, AWS was reported to be profitable, with sales of $1.57 billion in the first quarter of the year, and $265 million in operating income. Founder Jeff Bezos described it as a fast-growing $5 billion startup; analysts described it as *"surprisingly more profitable than forecast"*. In 2015, Gartner estimated that AWS customers are deploying 10x more infrastructure on AWS than the combined adoption of the next 14 cloud providers.

During the 2015 re: Invent keynote, AWS disclosed AWS had more than a million active customers every month in 190 countries, including nearly 2,000 government agencies, 5,000 education institutions and more than 17,500 nonprofits.

In 2016, AWS founder and Harvard Business School alumni Andy Jassy was named CEO of the division. In the first quarter of 2016, Amazon experienced a 42% rise in stock value because of increased earnings, of which AWS contributed 56% to the company's profit. During the fourth quarter of 2020, Andy Jassy was named CEO of Amazon.com to succeed founder Jeff Bezos. Here is my one second of fame being in the same picture frame as Amazon's CEO Andy Jassy along with the rest of the AWS Executive Team.

AWS generated $62 Billion in revenue for 2021. While Amazon is still profitable without AWS, AWS contributes to most of Amazon's operating profits. In 2021, Amazon generated almost $25 billion in operating profits with most profits coming from AWS.

New Era: The Future of Amazon Web Services

With the exceptional growth of AWS's business in recent years, AWS was beginning to attract some serious competition. The largest technology infrastructure providers felt like they were behind the 8 ball and playing catchup. Microsoft and Google demonstrated commitment to make the necessary investments to build their cloud businesses.

AWS was also starting to experience growing pains where its peculiar culture was being put to a test and stretching the boundaries of Amazon's leadership principles. Jeff Bezos created a unique culture at Amazon where all Amazonians lived and breathed the 14 leadership principles as a guiding compass in making everyday decisions from customer interactions, hiring decisions, and talent development.

AWS aligned and inherited Amazon's leadership principles and its culture to remain in harmony with the overall Amazon cultural identity. All decisions started from the customer and were worked backward including 90 to 95% of the service roadmaps at AWS being influenced based on customer feedback.

This level of commitment to customer obsession is what made Amazon a formidable competitor in all the industries it operated. Amazon's business models of creating flywheels which formed a vicious circle between customer adoption, low prices, operating at scale, lowering prices, and further customer adoption resulted in exponential growth in customer adoption, ever-increasing value creation for customers, and helped Amazon achieve scale and market leadership in the segments it chose to compete in.

The long-term orientation of Jeff Bezos' thinking is what made some investors nervous about short-term profitability and financial outcomes. Jeff believed that it took at least 7 years for a business to prove its feasibility before achieving growth. This long-term thinking trickled down to the hiring practices at Amazon wherein it took a long time to identify the candidates who could thrive in such a unique company culture.

At AWS, it took almost 160 days to hire one solution architect after rejecting at least 43 well-qualified candidates. Anyone hired into Amazon was considered a leader and could be safely assumed to be the best among the best based on the level of scrutiny in the hiring processes. There was ambiguity at multiple levels and by design. An ambiguity of role definition, the ambiguity of how decisions were made, and the ambiguity of how fast the technology evolved were considered normal and most Amazonians were numb to the volume of changes always happening around them.

Despite of all the internal challenges, AWS was growing gangbusters and competition started to heat up. One of the account teams in my territory reported, *"while we were stepping out of the customer meeting, we noticed it was Diane Green, CEO of Google Cloud, walking into the same conference room."* Later we discovered, Diane Green was there with a check book and ended up buying the customer's data center infrastructure.

What next?

I read these emerging competitive signals and dynamics as too interesting to miss and transitioned internally from solutions architecture to help and support building AWS's competitive intelligence function. Over the next three years (2017 to 2021), I had the most interesting experiences of my professional career competing with the most credible and smart competitors in the technology industry.

As cloud adoption was gaining momentum, the largest enterprise technology companies started to pay attention to AWS as a serious competitor. While during the first 5 to 7 beginning years AWS went unnoticed and competitor's made statements like cloud IaaS will fade away like any other hype. Now in 2017, it was no longer a secret that traditional enterprise technology companies like IBM, Oracle, Teradata, etc. were starting to lose customers to AWS. All large enterprise technology companies jumped in with all their money muscle to gain a slice of the cloud IaaS (Infrastructure as a Service) and PaaS (Platform as a Service) market.

Among these companies, the most serious contenders were Microsoft and Google. Both, Microsoft, and Google, played to their strengths to go after AWS as a competitor. Microsoft leveraged its enterprise customer base for Office 365, Microsoft Windows, and productivity tools like SharePoint and Power BI to move from on-premises to cloud. This involved a lot of deal-making and financial incentives for customers as well as partners to help these customers move to Microsoft Azure cloud. Microsoft even ran a play against AWS to attract retailers who were not so willing to spend money with their primary competitor Amazon.com.

On the other hand, Google approached the market with what it knew best including Google's strong foothold among marketers for search and advertising spend. Google cloud leveraged the power of Alphabet entities to package and sign long-term strategic partnerships with customers.

Google Ventures became active in investing in customers to buy the business. Google even leveraged its productivity suite namely G Suite including Gmail, Google meet, etc. to package deals with Google cloud customers.

Overall, what we can learn from these cloud wars is how companies like AWS leverage its mechanisms like flywheels to scale effectively.

PRINCIPLE THREE

LEVERAGE WISDOM OF THE CROWDS

BUILD COMMUNITIES

"Diversity and independence are important because the best collective decisions are the product of disagreement and contest, not consensus or compromise."
~ The Wisdom of Crowds by James Surowiecki

We live in a world today where communities overpower the experts. The diversity of thought in communities is well known to be far more valuable than the expert opinion of a select few experts. Though your company may have a few experts focusing on competitive intelligence or strategy, the cross-functional communities internally can be far more powerful in winning over the competition.

So how do you go about building internal cross-functional communities in an organization?

The first step involves identifying the key stakeholders across the different functions. Depending upon the size and scale of an organization, the functions you engage may vary. Some organizations early in their business journey may primarily have small teams of product, marketing, sales, and field engineering while some organizations which are further along in their maturity may have additional functions like Go-To-Market, Sales Strategy or Enablement.

Why do you need this competitive intelligence-focused community to span diverse functions? What specifically are you trying to accomplish by engaging these functions more closely?

The end goal is to cast a wider net so you could listen closely to a variety of different market signals from your competitors such as product announcements, new marketing campaigns, proof of concept landmines, or sales tactics.

Here are some specific objectives you are trying to accomplish by engaging these functions via this community:

- Product to help identify gaps in product capabilities.
- Go To Market to align with top sales campaigns.
- Sales enablement to disseminate compete assets.

- Field engineering to learn about customer decisions.
- Sellers to dive into why we win or lose to competition.
- Marketing to influence competitive messaging.

Let's dive into one of the real-world communities I had the opportunity to build.

Building a compete community at Amazon Web Services to take on Oracle

Two of my former employers, AWS and Oracle had, and even today continue to have, a very public and intense hate relationship. Fortunately, or unfortunately, I was in the middle of these technology giants going at each other.

During my tenure at AWS in 2018, I was assigned the challenging role at AWS to be a Global Competitive Intelligence lead with the first assignment to focus on Oracle. Why? Because customers were complaining about feeling helpless when it came to running their existing Oracle estates on-premises and were looking for ways to run their Oracle estates on the cloud or find alternatives. Customer obsession, as the key leadership principle at Amazon, was the guiding post to accept this challenge.

According to the leaders who hired me, there was no better person than me to lead this critical focus area mainly because previously I had spent eleven plus years at Oracle learning the tricks of the enterprise software trade. At Amazon, there is a famous saying, "*There is no compression algorithm for experience*".

In my opinion, both companies tend to be complete opposites when it comes to company culture, leadership styles, and competitive tone.

Oracle is perceived to be a bit aggressive given its strong sales culture over time while Amazon has built its brand around customer obsession. Oracle leaders typically did not shy away from taking a stab at competitors in public while AWS leaders typically avoided discussing competitors in public. Only exception being Andy Jassy (current Amazon CEO and former AWS's CEO) who over the years took multiple stabs at Oracle's (founder, former CEO, and current President/CTO) Larry Ellison during AWS re: Invent conference keynotes.

Here is an example from AWS re: Invent keynote delivered by Andy Jassy, taking a jab at Larry Ellison.

In addition to their differences in culture, leadership style, and competitive tone, both Oracle and AWS were aggressively pursuing each other's core business.

Between the years 2017 and 2019, AWS was trying to build a sustainable database business to push AWS and overall Amazon to higher profit margins and challenge Oracle at its core database software business. On the other hand, Oracle was entering cloud infrastructure turf to challenge AWS at its core competence.

While all this was going on, Amazon.com (the parent company of AWS), announced ambitious plans to move off Oracle software completely by 2020. There was an interesting dynamic between the two companies as Amazon.com was a customer of Oracle. Amazon.com used to be one of Oracle's top customers back in the day and famously ran some of the largest and mission critical business applications on Oracle database software. Amazon.com was also known to run one of the most challenging and scalable technology infrastructure in the world pushing the limits of technology.

This public announcement to pull the plug on Oracle software was a demonstration by Amazon to the entire world that it is possible to move off proprietary database software like Oracle to open-source alternatives, something that Amazon's cloud unit, AWS, proudly offered as a viable alternative to customers.

On the other hand, Larry was proudly claiming in the press that it will be very hard for Amazon to get off Oracle and still run its business at scale reliably on open-source alternatives.

In the meantime, Oracle announced its own ambitious plans to enter the cloud infrastructure space with Oracle Cloud Infrastructure. Oracle was challenging AWS with aggressively placed advertising and PR (Public Relations) campaigns like the one below at the bottom of this Wall Street Journal's front page.

Oracle was running a promotion for customers to share their AWS bill with Oracle where Oracle could potentially cut customer's AWS bill in half.

During the years I was in the role of Global compete lead for Oracle at AWS, AWS was clearly and even today continues to be the market leader in cloud infrastructure. On the other hand, Oracle was considered as a late entrant in cloud infrastructure market with Oracle Cloud Infrastructure (OCI). At first, Oracle's CEO at the time Larry Ellison ignored the term cloud computing as a hype, later he changed his mind to say he agreed more with AWS's definition of the cloud than Salesforce.com's version or IBM's version of the cloud. Finally, around 2016 or so, Oracle announced its own version of AWS's cloud infrastructure.

As a late entrant, Oracle was substantially behind in terms of features, capabilities, and security and compliance accreditations. Also, Oracle in its history had always gravitated towards higher margin businesses like enterprise software and support services except for the time it acquired Sun Microsystems.

On April 16, 2009 Thursday afternoon at 12:02 pm, I was driving from one of the buildings to another at Oracle headquarters in Redwood Shores, California. Suddenly, I find my car stuck between two limousines outside Oracle conference center. Someone wearing blue jeans and black t-shirt stepped out the limousine and walked into the conference center. An unusually tall lady in a formal suit followed him and she was holding a stack of files in her hands. An hour later, I was pulling my car out Oracle conference center parking where someone ran across behind my car. It was Charles Phillips, Oracle's President. Chasing her down was her administrative assistant. Again, she was holding a stack of files. On Monday April 20, 2009, Oracle announced its intention to acquire Sun Microsystems for $7.4 billion. The months prior IBM was in talks with Sun Microsystems however both could not settle on a price. Sun Microsystems owned Java which was critical to IBM's technology stack. That Monday morning, I realized that the person who stepped out the limousine was Scott McNeally, Sun Microsystems's Founder and CEO. That meeting at Oracle conference center was about Oracle acquiring Sun Microsystems.

Coming back to the year 2018 and Oracle's track record at over indexing on higher margin businesses. This pursuit of Oracle to build cloud infrastructure to compete with AWS was seen by industry as a sign of desperation and being left behind in the cloud. Such capital-intensive business of cloud infrastructure with building and operating data centers at scale was a new muscle for Oracle. But Oracle had little choice since cloud adoption had taken off and customers started frequently questioning Oracle's credibility in cloud infrastructure space.

AWS was a meaningfully, much better choice for customers moving to the cloud because AWS had the longest experience (over 10 years), more services, more functionality within those services, a faster pace of innovation, a bigger footprint, more highly available applications, better security, and an extensive ecosystem of cloud partners.

Fortune 10,000 enterprise companies were and even today run massive Oracle estates to run their business. As many of these large enterprises embarked on the journey to move the cloud, they were looking at AWS for guidance on how to move legacy Oracle workloads to AWS or find suitable replacements.

As Andy Jassy, at the time AWS's CEO and now Amazon's CEO, famously quotes in his AWS re: Invent keynote address in 2019,

"When companies move to the cloud, it is like moving your house. You may decisions like what to put on that mover's truck and what to leave behind".

To block customers from moving their Oracle estates to AWS, Oracle started spreading FUD (Fear, Uncertainty, and Doubt) that customers are not legally allowed to run Oracle software on AWS cloud infrastructure. Either customers would have to pay double in Oracle licensing fee on AWS or customers may not receive critical ongoing support services from Oracle if they chose to run Oracle software on AWS infrastructure.

Least to say, I had a herculean task ahead of me. On one hand, the goal was to help customers break free from proprietary lock in with Oracle and on the other hand, it was to help them peacefully run Oracle software on AWS infrastructure. Not to forget, the task was also to block Oracle from becoming a serious threat to AWS in the cloud infrastructure space.

When I started reading the context internally at AWS, there was no structured team focused on helping customers with moving or running Oracle workloads on AWS. Field teams at AWS were struggling in Oracle competitive situations to engage the right resources.

The AWS field sales teams had scaled to tens of thousands of field sellers and solution architects globally in 2018 however there was no way the lean but mighty function of competitive intelligence will scale to that extend in headcount. This concept of single threaded leadership became a forcing function to invent new and creative ways to scale yourself.

Jeff Bezos always preached the notion that, *"good intentions don't scale, only mechanisms scale"*. The objective was to build scaling mechanisms so these efforts could all deliver broader and bigger impact across the company and the industry at large. Specifically, the efforts to help customers run Oracle on AWS, to break free from Oracle lock-in, and to stop Oracle cloud infrastructure from becoming a serious competitive threat.

To offer a seamless AWS experience to customers, one of the mechanisms was to create a global Oracle community with geographic and organizational representation across different business units, functions, and geographies.

It was a grass roots effort to find like-minded people who deeply cared about the pains customers were experiencing. I was always traveling to different global geographical regions to meet with top customers or prospects in the region, learn about the regional blockers, and enabling the local customers and field leaders on how to unblock these challenges.

In the process of these global travels, I met with like-minded individuals in the field who deeply cared about these blockers and were willing to step up to help be the regional voice connected to headquarters.

Within 6 months, we had 42 such like-minded individuals who passionately wanted to contribute and be part of this global Oracle community. Oracle community acted as a pseudo TFC (Technical Field Community) and met on a quarterly basis to review voice of the customer, feedback from the field, top areas of concern, roadmap updates, and PFR (Product Feature Requests). E.g., Oracle community catered to customer demand for specialized Oracle technical depth which helped AWS earn trust to win these competitive deals. Community created content repositories, accelerated PFRs, delivered technical thought leadership in the form of whitepapers, and customer references.

We knew it was working when AWS won a massive competitive Oracle workload. In this competitive situation, on one side was Oracle's CEO Safra Catz and on the other hand, one of our front-line community members. Despite of the executive presence and pressure on the customer, customer chose to run their entire Oracle estate on AWS.

Also, when the trajectory of AWS database business was in a positive direction as depicted below. AWS went from rank 7 in 2013 to being number 1 in 2023, surpassing Oracle and Microsoft in the category of Database Management Systems.

Gartner DBMS Market Share Ranks: 2011-2022

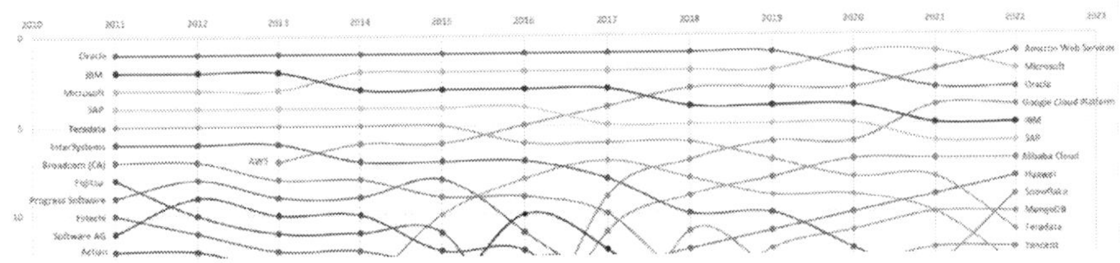

Credits: Adam Ronthal, VP Analyst at Gartner

PRINCIPLE FOUR

MASTER COOPETITION

RECONCILING CUSTOMER OBSESSION WITH COMPETING

Leaders start with the customer and work backward. They work vigorously to earn and keep customer trust. Although leaders pay attention to competitors, they obsess over customers.
~ Amazon's leadership principle 'Customer Obsession'

We operate our businesses in a complex world. A world where clear boundaries of competition and cooperation just do not exist. As a result, we tend to compete and collaborate with the same business entities at the same time. Just imagine you are Apple where on one hand your biggest competitor is Samsung in the smartphone segment while on the other hand your largest iPhone display supplier is Samsung.

Many, if not most, businesses are in a similar dilemma. 'How to reconcile customer obsession with competing?'. If you are experiencing similar feelings, you have picked up the right book. As a former employee of Amazon, I faced the exact dilemma described above. While Amazon's #1 leadership principle is customer obsession, it finds itself in such situations all the time.

Customer obsession is cited as a company philosophy by most companies however put into practice by only a few. To share an example, in the early 2000s during Christmas weekend, the most popular Christmas gift at the time was the Apple iPod. Amazon was receiving lots of orders of Apple iPods however Apple could not fulfill the demand. As a result, one of the procurement managers at

Amazon decided to demonstrate the highest level of customer obsession. Ignoring what impact his decision would have on profit margins, he decided to drive into each Apple store within the proximity of where he lived and bought iPods at full retail store price and fulfilled most of the pending orders for customers.

What we can learn from this real-world event is that such a decision will be frowned upon by most companies. Perhaps, this decision could have been a career-limiting move for this employee at another company, however celebrated at a company that values customer obsession above all.

During an Amazon wide All Hands, I had the opportunity to submit a live question for Jeff Bezos. I asked, *"We, as Amazon, offer products and services which sometimes collaborate and sometimes compete with the same entities. How should Amazon think about coopetition?"*. To make his point, Bezos shared an example of coopetition between Netflix and Amazon Prime. *"Just imagine our situation at Amazon where on one hand AWS is working super hard to make Netflix successful while on another hand Amazon operates its own movie streaming service, Amazon Prime Video. We must learn how to do both, in parallel, effectively because customers love choice. "*

Across different businesses, Amazon collaborates and competes with different companies. E.g., Amazon's core online store competes with the retailers likes of Walmart, Alibaba, Flipcart, and Target while some of the retailers' partner on Amazon to leverage things like Amazon Pay or Fulfillment by Amazon. Similarly, Amazon Web Services competes with the likes of Microsoft Azure, and Google Cloud. AWS also offers services that overlap with several Independent Software Vendors (ISVs) that also run their business on AWS. E.g., MongoDB, Snowflake to name a few.

Overall, it is the new normal in business. Something that we all must master to offer choice to customers.

Below is a breakdown of Amazon's revenue model and its competitors in each of the businesses. Credits: Visual Capitalists

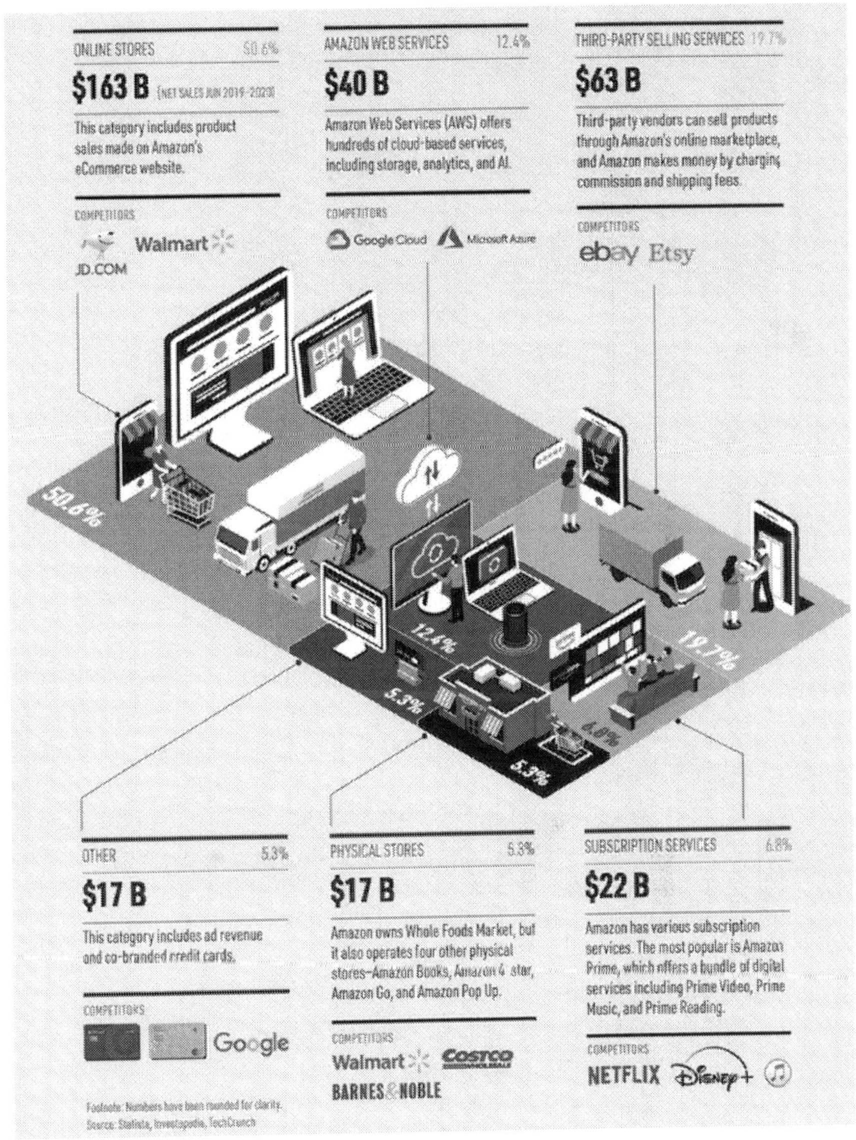

Coopetition -- also spelled co-opetition -- is a portmanteau, combining the words cooperation and competition. Competitive businesses that also cooperate when it is to their advantage are said to be in coopetition.

The principles and practices of coopetition are credited to New York University and Yale business professors Adam M.

Brandenburger and Barry J. Nalebuff. They introduced the principles and practices of coopetition in their book Co-opetition, first published in 1996.

Coopetition is a business strategy that uses insights gained from game theory to understand when it is better for competitors to work together. Coopetition games are mathematical models used to examine in what ways cooperation among competitors can increase the benefits to all players and grow the market. The models also examine when it's best to allow competition to divide the existing benefits among players to provide the leading competitors with more market share.

The goal of coopetition strategy is to move the competitors away from a zero-sum game, in which the winner takes all and losers are left empty-handed. The Value Net Model replaces the approach of a zero-sum game with a plus-sum game. In it, the result is profitable for all the competitors when they work together.

Take for example Pfizer and BioNTech. The March 2020 agreement between Pfizer and BioNTech to jointly develop a COVID-19 vaccine is an example of coopetition. The agreement enabled the two pharmaceutical companies to combine development and manufacturing capabilities. As a result, they were able to get the vaccine to market by the end of 2020 and have produced hundreds of millions of doses in 2021.

The promise of coopetition as a strategy is to reduce costs, avoid duplication of effort, and make the pie bigger for both competitors involved. As you assess the situation of whether to partner with a competitor, it is important to consider the ramifications of not partnering. What happens if you do not partner? Will the competitor partner with another common competitor putting you at a disadvantage? Who has more bargaining power, you, or competitor, in such a coopetition arrangement?

Take, for example, Samsung and Apple. Both compete fiercely for the smartphone market, yet Apple represents 30%+ of Samsung's revenues for smartphone screens. If Samsung would have decided not to cooperate and sell smartphone screens to Apple, it could have put Samsung at an advantage in the long term for smartphone market share, yet Apple could have decided to partner with a common third competitor in such a situation. This could have resulted in Samsung losing this additional revenue stream selling screens to Apple.

There are also several such examples where competitors form sort of a duopoly like Coca Cola and Pepsi. Even if one of the two invests in active marketing of black sugar water, both benefit as a category. Notice, there is no clear third competitor. It varies based on who you ask or which region you are in.

Though all matches are not created equal, one competitor may have a significantly more competitive advantage over another. In such situations too, the stronger of the two benefits from staying away from the Federal Trade Commission's radar for anti-competitive practices while the weaker of the two benefits from the partnership to gain access to customers and distribution channels it would have otherwise taken years to build on its own.

Keep in mind that making coopetition strategy work for you requires a lot more than just establishing a partnership with a competitor. It requires a major mindset shift for your internal stakeholders to adjust to the new arrangement. It takes a cultural shift to move from competing to assessing customer situations to decipher whether it is in your best interest to compete or collaborate.

As a result, some companies establish coopetition tenets to navigate such ambiguous situations. You may ask, *"Mayur, what is a tenet?"* A tenet, by definition, is a principle or belief, especially one of the main principles of a religion or philosophy. Think of tenets as guiding principles for your internal staff on how to operate directionally given the situation. Coopetition tenets help your internal staff read the context better to determine whether to compete or collaborate in each customer situation.

Let's dive deeper into one of the real-world coopetition stories the world had the opportunity to witness in the recent past.

ChatGPT Creator OpenAI: To Compete or To Cooperate

ChatGPT's powerful capability and viral adoption of reaching 1 million users in 5 days have been marked as a new milestone in the development of AI/ML.

Formed in 2015, OpenAI's original mission as a non-profit was to build safe AI technology for the benefit of humanity. I remember Open AI reaching out to my team at AWS asking for free cloud credits as a non-profit.

The startup's organizational structure was modified in 2019 to allow it to raise billions of dollars — mostly from Microsoft — and the firm now makes money by charging a subscription for access to its powerful generative AI tools, including the popular ChatGPT bot, and licensing its large language models (LLMs) to businesses.

While on one hand Open AI raised more than $10 billion from its partner Microsoft, on the other hand Open AI is not owned by Microsoft and has continued to develop partnerships that arm other companies with its AI solutions.

In a way, Microsoft and OpenAI are both cooperating and competing at the same time.

Microsoft is one of the biggest beneficiaries of the ChatGPT revolution. Microsoft plans to and has embedded Chat GPT across its own software product line and offers it as an Azure service. One can easily see ChatGPT writing emails in Outlook, creating drafts in Microsoft Word, generating texts and images in PowerPoint, coordinating Team Meetings, assisting queries in Power BI, and being embedded in business applications like Dynamics CRM and ERP.

Microsoft shocked the broader world (and its competitor Google) by integrating OpenAI's state-of-the-art large language model into Bing (Microsoft's search engine), via a chatbot named Sydney. During these integrations, Microsoft employees have expressed resentment that that their own employer has begun overlooking its internal AI projects in favor of OpenAI. Another point of contention is that most of Microsoft has no access to the inner workings of GPT, or OpenAI's tech. This has left Microsoft teams and researchers out in the cold, despite the $10 billion plus Microsoft investment in Open AI. This has become an even bigger point of content since OpenAI started telling Microsoft to slow down the integration of ChatGPT in Bing, citing the risks of releasing an untrained chatbot.

At the same time, OpenAI has developed its own products and API services that appeal to the same customers Microsoft is courting. ChatGPT also competes with Bing AI. There is a lingering confusion as both companies' sales teams end up pitching to the same customers. Also, OpenAI has continued to develop partnerships that arm other companies with its AI solutions. For example, Salesforce now offers a ChatGPT-infused product that directly competes with OpenAI-driven features in Microsoft's own business software. This includes things like Salesforce partnering with OpenAI to launch Einstein GPT. The content generator directly competes with Microsoft Office's new suite of features. This has led the two companies, both Microsoft and Salesforce, to ship similar products, powered by the same technology - OpenAI ChatGPT.

Despite these challenges, Open AI's ChatGPT, has reached an impressive 200 million monthly users.

Such complex coopetition dynamics commonly exists across the technology industry where on one hand you work hard to make the partnership work and on other hand, you compete directly with your partner for the same customers. Only time will tell how such complex coopetition dynamics evolve in the future.

PRINCIPLE FIVE

SHAPE THE NARRATIVE

To articulate the importance of "Shaping the Narrative" in competitive rivalries, let's discuss the sequence of events with the famous Joint Enterprise Defense Infrastructure (JEDI) contract.

Let's dive deeper into one of the real-world narratives shaping I had the opportunity to witness. The facts available are from public sources, respecting the confidentially of my previous employer.

Shaping the Narrative for JEDI: High Stakes Game of $10 Billion Defense Contract

The Joint Enterprise Defense Infrastructure (JEDI) contract was a large United States DoD (Department of Defense) cloud computing contract reported as being worth $10 billion over ten years.

Controversy

Companies interested in the contract were Amazon, Google, Microsoft, and Oracle. After protests from Google employees, Google decided to drop out of contention for the contract because of conflict with its corporate values. The deal was considered "gift-wrapped for Amazon" until Oracle (co-chaired by Safra Catz) contested the contract, citing the National Defense Authorization Act over IDIQ contracts and the conflicts of interest from Deap Ubhi, who worked for Amazon both before and after his time in the Department of Defense. This led Eric G. Bruggink, senior judge of the United States Court of Federal Claims, to place the contract award on hold.

In August 2019, weeks before the winner was expected to be announced, President Donald Trump ordered the contract placed on hold again for Defense Secretary Mark Esper to investigate complaints of favoritism towards Amazon. In October 2019, it was announced that the contract was awarded to Microsoft. Media has noted Trump's dislike towards Amazon's founder, Jeff Bezos, owner of the Washington Post, a newspaper critical of Trump. According to Bezos, Trump "used his power to 'screw Amazon' out of the JEDI Contract". The JEDI contract was awarded to Microsoft on October 25, 2019, the DoD announced, but AWS filed documents with the Court of Federal Claims on November 22, 2019, challenging the award; its legal strategy included calling Trump to testify.

A federal judge, Patricia Campbell-Smith, halted Microsoft's work on the project on February 13, 2020, a day before the system was scheduled to go live, awaiting a resolution in Amazon's suit. She said that Amazon's claims are reasonable and "is likely to succeed on the merits of its argument that the DOD improperly evaluated" Microsoft's offer. As a result, the DOD was forced by a federal judge to reopen bidding for the contract. In the wake of that reopening, Amazon had filed additional protests related to modifications which have been made to selected sections of the contract. DOD legal filings had stated that the final award of the contract cannot take place until at least August 17, and may yet be delayed beyond that date as well. On September 4, 2020, the Department of Defense reaffirmed that Microsoft won the JEDI Cloud contract after the reevaluation of the proposal, stating that Microsoft's proposal continues to represent the best value to the government.

The JEDI contract with Microsoft was cancelled on July 6, 2021, with the expectation that a new program called "Joint Warfighter Cloud Capability" (JWCC) would replace it, which would involve services from multiple vendors. On November 19, 2021, the Department of Defense issued formal solicitations to four of the original JEDI companies: Amazon, Google, Microsoft, and Oracle; notably not including the fifth provider consulted, IBM.

Outcome

On December 7, 2022, the JWCC contract was awarded to the four companies for a combined total of up to $9 billion under the program.

PRINCIPLE SIX

AVOID PRICE WARS

FIGHT OR FLIGHT

In the battle to win the hearts and minds of customers, companies tend to frequently leverage price as a lever. Whether you ask this question to a customer in 2033 or even in 2053, *"would you like lower prices?"*; the answer most likely is going to be a yes. This is one of those constants in time you could build your business around however *"is price the only thing you want to hang your hat on?"*.

The bigger question is "who emerges as a winner in a price war?". Typically, in the short term, the initial winner emerges to the be the customer benefiting from the frequent price reductions by the competitors. In the mid to long term, customer sometimes ends up being the loser because price wars frequently kill competitors resulting in more pricing power getting consolidated in the hands of select few providers.

Price wars are common and have emerged more commonly in some industries compared to others. These industries tend to have an industry structure with a few companies dominating the industry. These industries also tend to have the characteristics of either offering commoditized products/services or being capital intensive.

E.g., airline and telecom industries are the one's among the hardest hit by price wars in recent history. Price wars in the airline industry emerged in the early 90s when airlines in the US reduced fares drastically to match or undercut the competitors. The outcome? Massive increase in air traffic with massive losses due to eroded profit margins. The airline industry has never been the same since. The competitive price dynamics change approximately every 6 minutes for airlines these days. Look at the telecom operator price wars of the late 90s where the long-distance call rates were slashed one after the other by top US telecom providers.

Let's dive deeper into one of the real-world price wars I had the opportunity to experience first-hand.

Telecom Price Wars and The Race to Zero - Palta Infocomm

Behind a giant wooden executive desk of a small telecom company, I was pondering on a decision whether to continue running my 3-year-old telecom startup or to throw in the towel. We were in the middle of a fierce price war between global telecom giants trying to capture almost close to a billion plus subscribers in India.

In my humble opinion, "there is nothing called a failure, either you succeed, or you learn". What I am about to share are lessons I learned the hard way by making numerous mistakes while building a business.

The meta lesson learned is all about price wars and other lessons learned are related to science (economics, market research, technology, finance, industry structure, competitive strategy) and some related to art (customer acquisition focus and retention, talent management, balancing long term vs short term goals).

My intent is to pull some important business lessons from the real world into perspective for learning purposes. Also, my hope is perhaps someone would be able to walk away with some meaning takeaways in not repeating the same mistakes I made. To net it out, try to capture as much value as you can.

Wireline and Wireless Price Wars in India - The Race to Zero

Telecommunications industry was in the middle of commoditization in India in the early 2000s when big 800-pound gorillas were competing for each new subscriber while trying to retain existing subscribers. Big established players like BSNL, Airtel, Orange, and Reliance were fiercely competing on price and willing to cut their margins drastically in response to competitive price pressures. Acquiring each new subscriber meant spreading out their fixed-cost investments over more volume of subscribers.

My business model at Palta Infocomm centered around setting up a small-scale city-wide wireline telecom optic network infrastructure from the ground up in one of the urban cities of Northern India.

The scope of the project was to start small at a city level and if the pilot project succeeds, expand the network subsequently to an entire state with a market size of 23 million subscribers spanning 22,000 miles. To accomplish this, we partnered with Reliance Communications (among the top 10 companies in India by market capitalization at the time). In this business arrangement, Reliance would sell a bulk volume of calls to us and gain from our experiences piloting an entry into this hypercompetitive market. We had complete autonomy from owning and setting up all the telecom and fiber optic infrastructure, acquiring subscribers and reselling a large volume of calls bought upfront from Reliance Communications.

The key business lesson learned here is that never start with investing all your own money if the upfront fixed capital costs are super high, it is wiser to raise capital than play with your own money. However, the venture capitalist scene was non-existent, and we ended up taking a bank loan.

Some of the unknowns to me in this business opportunity were uncertainty of consumer demand, subscriber's willingness to pay, barriers to entry, competitor's variable costs, and potential service disruption issues that frequently pop-up in running a telecom operation as a service, customer satisfaction issues, billing errors, collections, and service disruptions due to lack of electricity in the region.

Looking back, these were also majority of the mistakes I made in reading the context and assessing the future impact of my choices. Another important thing to note is that technology was slowly shifting to wireless mobile phones. This is around the time when Motorola and Nokia introduced there heavy and now relatively ugly looking mobile phones in the market. The costs of making mobile phone calls were dropping from approximately 33 cents a minute (converted to US Dollars for ease of understanding) to 1 cent a minute. This meant war, a classic price war where players with the most money muscle may survive while others pack up their bags and leave.

High fixed costs and the break-even point

Telecom wireline business is a high fixed-cost business with upfront capital investments of telephone exchanges, expensive optic fiber connecting endpoints between customers, and the fixed costs of installing optic fiber between endpoints. The primary upside was the promising future of internet and data usage.

The same Optic fiber could deliver internet data as well as cable entertainment in the long term over the same network of wired connections; however, the potential uses of the investment were far ahead of its time. Keeping the investments and potential volume of subscribers in mind, it would have taken between 5 to 7 years to break even from the upfront investments.

Telecom is in some ways like operating an airline with high upfront capital investments and in some cases establishing long term contracts among major players and network providers.

Lesson learned: If your break-even is not in the first 18 months, preferably the first 6 to 9 months, you may want to rethink about the opportunity again, unless you are Amazon and have access to endless venture capital. This is where the concept of opportunity cost is key, thinking through the cost of capital and the other business opportunities you may forgo to choose one is worth it.

Market entrant and the prior confusion of average Vs fixed costs among competitors

I missed a very important point in focusing on variable costs in pricing and ignoring sunk costs. Instead, I kept accounting for the total costs (fixed costs and variable costs) in my pricing decisions. As an entrant into a very capital-intensive industry of telecom, I was trying to recover my high fixed costs while the currently established players in the market, some multinational, some state-owned with $10 Billion+ on their balance sheets were willing to even price below their variable costs to gain economies of scale with subscribe market share.

Money muscle and competitive responses

Exactly what I feared happened, wireless technology entered the market and gained traction. Wireline technology became almost obsolete since a better, faster, a more convenient substitute was readily available at lower costs. In response to this, most big players lowered their prices offering free calls with monthly commitments.

Most wireline providers like BSNL and MTNL were offering these services at approximately 4 cents a minute and the time to subscribe to a new service meant long wait times due to the government nature of these state-owned entities. Customer service across these competitive services was generally poor. These services were so well penetrated in the market that even an invoice from these state-owned entities was accepted as a proof of address for legal work.

My pricing was simple 1-tier pricing, pay an upfront fee of $9.99 to get started and a $9.99 monthly subscription thereafter with no commitments, first 200 calls were offered for free, per call charges were 3 cents, and within network Reliance to Reliance wireline calls at the state level free. This meant two subscribers with this service could consume unlimited calls without incurring any additional cost. Wireless carriers lowered the prices to 1 cent per minute and I experienced a huge subscriber churn. Big players continued to compete fiercely while I knew it was time to close shop.

What we can learn from this real-world story is that price wars are real. As business leaders, we must take the time to think through and deliberately assess the downstream impact and implications of playing this game of lowering prices to gain customers. Also, make sure you are not the one initiating this game.

Hopefully, the next time your sales teams come to you for approving discounts to uncut competitor's price, you are reminded of this story.

PRINCIPLE SEVEN

CHANGE THE RULES OF THE GAME

CREATE A NEW CATEGORY

Business is a very competitive and aggressive sport. As business leaders, we must be on our toes all the time to learn the everchanging rules of the game very quickly and adjust accordingly.

Many times, in business you have little control over the rules of the game. You may be dealt with cards that you don't like however should you continue to play with the cards? or should you try to influence and change the rules of the game?

Let's dive deeper into one of the real-world categories I had the opportunity to create.

New Category Creation: ICI Carbon

The year was 2001, I was living in India in a small town of Punjab, a northern state of India. My family was operating a business in chemical manufacturing since 1973. Majority of our customers used our chemical called carbon black as a key raw material to manufacture rubber products like car tires, footwear, or plastics. There were close to 321 footwear manufacturing units in Punjab, and we had approximately 32% share of the market. Business was growing double digits each year.

During the season of Diwali, an auspicious festival of lights and prosperity in Indian culture, our business historically generated 25% of our annual revenue. As this festive season approach in 2001, we heard that approximately 297 of the 321 customers that manufactured footwear were in the process of closing their manufacturing operations due to competition from China. A sudden influx of Chinese made footwear entered the Indian market which offered half the cost and twice the durability. Majority of our customers were going to suddenly disappear over the next 3 months and the remainder were scaling down their manufacturing output to reduce their inventory levels and to cut down these losses.

In the middle of this chaos, one of the prospects from a different state in India and from a different industry all together ordered a small quantity of our product. Out of curiosity, I reached out to this customer via a cold call.

He picked up the phone and didn't say anything while I heard loud noises of machines in the background. *"Yes, tell me"*, he said. I politely greeted this customer and expressed curiosity to learn about his business and how he planned to use our chemical in his manufacturing process. We arranged for a lunch meeting, and I flew to see this person in flesh.

As we were waiting for a server at a fine restaurant, I asked this person what types of products he was manufacturing. He said, *"We manufacture powder coatings which is the powder form of paint and is more durable to apply in industrial applications"*.

My next question was, *"How do you plan to use our chemical grade in manufacturing powder coatings? Also, our chemical is carbon black and primarily offered black color, how can you make other colors from it?"*. He smiled and said, *"Black is the most popular color in the Indian market and our grade offered exceptional Jetness to his powder coatings"*.

He said, *"If you are willing to invest in R&D and iterate over the surface chemistry of your grades, you could own this market. Currently, the top players in this segment across India are companies from Germany and US. As a result, their grades cost a fortune and most powder manufacturers don't afford to use them because these high costs of raw materials erode their margins, given the end customers in Indian market are quite cost sensitive."*

I was quickly scrambling to take notes on a paper napkin. In the back of mind, I was thinking about the current situation back home and how we were almost at risk of closing the business that had a solid run from 28 years from 1973 to 2001. As a kid growing up, my teachers and elders always instilled the hunger for knowledge in me and deeply ingrained the value of endless curiosity to seek the truth.

I was not too sure how much to trust the advice of this customer. Trusting this advice would mean significant departure from the past focus on footwear and major capital investments in R&D to break new ground in a target market segment that we had no knowledge of. At the lunch table, I filled up several napkins full of notes from the meeting and flew back home that evening.

During a 45-minute lunch conversation, I discovered that though the set of chemical properties that paint manufacturing required were different, they were attainable with specific R&D efforts. So, I took the specific set of requirements back to my team which consisted of 6 individuals, only 2 of them were technically sound chemical engineers, while rest were more manufacturing and sales focused. We took a step back to assess and evaluate the requirements and see whether these were enough feasible. The requirements were high Jetness measured by electron microscopy, oil absorption measured by a dilution test of under 50, tinting strength of above 100, lead free substance, UV resistance for durability measured by 400 hours of exposure to UV rays.

If we did not pivot to these new set of requirements, we were going to be out of business in less than 6 months because we had only less than 5% of the customers left to serve and high overheads of manufacturing to manage.

The initial scope was to give it a try. I was curious how far could we get in meeting these technical requirements. We made some major changes to the manufacturing process such as quality of carbon feedstock, temperature controls, drying process, etc. Identified a paint manufacturer through friends who would keep these trials discreet. Launched a proof of concept with these new set of requirements and we were a 43% match, over the next couple of months, we demonstrated tenacity in tweaking the chemical properties and went back to several customers one at a time.

We had finally reached an 87% match in requirements. Then, I launched an active campaign with my team, hired 2 chemists to visit customers for 84 Proof of concepts. Only 36 of these succeeded and it was a time-consuming process of submitting samples, doing RFPs, scheduling time, traveling, and getting their buy-in. So, I went to several customers and dug deeper into what common set of criteria do they deem a success for such proof of concepts, and we agreed on top 3 namely, Jetness, Oil Absorption, and Tinting Strength.

Then, I identified a research institute who would offer us these 3 certifications with an extensive testing by their team of scientist. We cut short the POC time. As a result, the sales cycles accelerated, and the 3 certifications provided the proof points.

Once the proof of technical feasibility was there, I shifted my focus to understand the competition and to identify where we fit in this market landscape. On one hand were the high quality but expensive grades from companies in Germany and US. On the other hand, were low-quality low-priced grades made in India whose primary target was not even paints or powder coatings. These served the high-volume markets of tires, rubber products, and plastics.

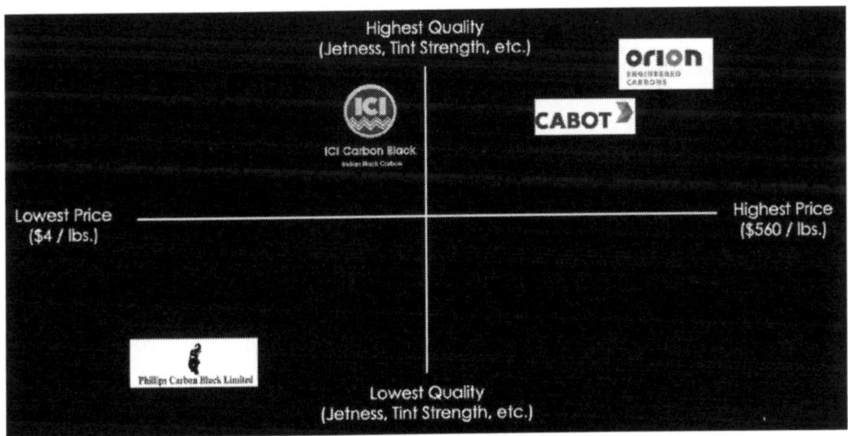

Clearly, I could see a gap in the market that I could fill. This led to the creation of a new category - specialty carbon black grades for paints & powder coatings. These offered high quality - as good as the most expensive grades from our German and American competitors - however at less than a third the price.

Over the next 6 months, we defined this new category and educated the industry. Our customer base grew from 36 customers to 167 customers in 18 months and owned a healthy 16% share of the market. We were back in business. This business continues to thrive even today and celebrated its 50-year anniversary in 2023.

Little did I know that what I went through as an experience was the process of category creation. Over the years, I worked at companies like Amazon Web Services which defined a new category of infrastructure cloud computing. I was unfamiliar with this term until I read the book - Category Creation - by Anthony Kennada.

In his book, Anthony defines:

Category creation is a business strategy that focuses on positioning and evangelizing a brand-new problem observed in the marketplace, in addition to the solution for that very problem.

PART III

BEING

Being a competitive strategist

MEET THE MOST PROMINENT COMPETITIVE STRATEGISTS

Around the 5th century BCE in ancient China, Sun Tzu offered his timeless advice on military strategy and tactics. As a Chinese military general, strategist, and philosopher, Sun Tzu is best known for his influential book "The Art of War," which has been applied to other fields, such as business and politics, and is considered one of the most important works on strategy ever written. Sun Tzu's teachings emphasize the importance of understanding the enemy, adapting to changing circumstances, and achieving victory through superior tactics and planning.

Among Sun Tzu's principles, the one that remains at the core of businesses even today is, "Know yourself and know your enemy". He prescribes that it is critical for victory that you invest the time, energy, and resources to understand your own strengths and weaknesses as well as those of your opponent.

Around the 4th century BCE in ancient India, Chanakya offered the earliest works on economics, politics, and statecraft in the world through his influential book "Arthashastra". Chanakya, also known as Kautilya or Vishnugupta, was an ancient Indian teacher, philosopher, and royal advisor. His legacy includes the Maurya Empire, one of the largest and most powerful empires in ancient India, which he helped to establish and advise under the reign of Emperor Chandragupta Maurya.

Chanakya is known for his practical advice on diplomacy and strategy, including the use of spies, deception, and alliances in political and military affairs. Despite his pragmatic approach to governance, Chanakya also emphasized the importance of ethics and morality in leadership, including the virtues of honesty, justice, and compassion.

Chanakya believed in the importance of education and personal development and is credited with founding one of the earliest universities in India, Takshashila.

Around the same time in history, Vishnu Sharma composed the Panchatantra, an ancient collection of animal fables and tales from India. The earliest version of the text is thought to have been written in Sanskrit, an ancient Indian language that continues to be studied till present day. Vishnu Sharma was a learned Brahmin scholar and advisor who was tasked with teaching the sons of a king important moral and political lessons.

The tales are primarily meant to impart moral and ethical lessons through the actions of animals, often anthropomorphized and given human-like characteristics. These tales were known as the Panchatantra, which translates to "Five Principles" in Sanskrit. The Panchatantra explores a range of moral and ethical issues, such as the dangers of greed and selfishness, the importance of loyalty and friendship, and the consequences of deception and betrayal. The stories often feature clever characters who use their wit and intelligence to overcome challenges and obstacles, and who ultimately triumph over their adversaries through their virtues and moral strength.

Like Sun Tzu, Chanakya, and Vishnu Sharma, there have been many strategists in history who have left their mark on strategy in different times and under different circumstances. Some famous examples are:

- Alexander the Great: The ancient Greek king and military commander who conquered vast territories across Asia and Europe, using innovative tactics and strategies.

- Julius Caesar: The Roman general and statesman who is known for his military conquests, political and administrative reforms, and literary works such as "The Gallic Wars."

- Napoleon Bonaparte: The French military and political leader who conquered much of Europe in the early 19th century, using innovative tactics and strategies such as the "Napoleonic Code" and the "Grand Army."

- Miyamoto Musashi: The Japanese swordsman and philosopher who is known for his book "The Book of Five Rings," which outlines his philosophy of martial arts and strategy.

- Carl von Clausewitz: The Prussian general and military theorist who is known for his book "On War," which is considered one of the most important works on military strategy and philosophy.

Though there has been lots of literature and textbooks on competition and strategy, the world we live in today is drastically different than what some of these historic strategists may have ever imagined. Business leaders need new thinking and new ways to approach the important topic of competition to keep up with today's uncertain times. In this book, business leaders will get introduced to the novel Outcompete Operating System, how to apply the Outcompete Model, and seven strategic principles that they can apply to their businesses to gain lasting competitive advantage.

PLAYING TO YOUR STRENGTHS

Competitive differentiation is about applying your strengths to your competitor's weaknesses.

The phrase "David and Goliath" has taken on a more popular meaning denoting an underdog situation, a contest wherein a smaller, weaker opponent faces a much bigger, stronger adversary. Even if David was relatively smaller in size and strength, David's strength as a shepherd was his slingshot skills to shepherd the herd of sheep. David was asked to wear armor to protect him against the mighty blows of Goliath however David knew that his strength was being quick on his feet and if he chose to wear armor, it may slow him down. On the other hand, Goliath's strength was his size and strength. David recognized Goliath's weakness was his exposed forehead and relatively slow speed so his slingshot to Goliath's forehead was like applying his strength to his opponent's weakness.

By playing to your strengths, you can develop them even more and become a unique professional or grow your personal abilities as well beyond the average. By becoming much more successful at what we do best, we can reach new heights.

While competing in business, your customer may hire your company for a specific job to be done while your customer may hire another company (could be your direct or indirect competitor) for another job to be done. The real question remains whether your company and its executives have a true picture of why customers choose your company or its product/service over competitors.

- Do you really have fact-based knowledge of why you win against or lose to competitors?

- What set of activities do you perform on a frequent basis to seek inputs from your customer about your company, your product, your staff, and how you stack up against your top competitors?

Uncovering your strengths is like a truth-seeking mission where you are being vocally critical about your company's strengths and weaknesses compared to alternatives. One of the many ways companies uncover their strengths and areas of growth is through the voice of the customer. Customers tend to decide with their money whether your product/service adds value to their business or whether a competitor's product/service does.

Though we may hire the smartest engineers or product managers, customers are the ultimate decision-makers, and it is critical to establish mechanisms to continuously work backward from the voice of the customer. Some companies have formal customer advisory boards while some hire third parties to survey their customers and capture the voice of the customer. There are pros and cons to each approach.

While a customer or product advisory board gives the opportunity for your engineers/product teams to engage with customers and seek feedback, the quality of feedback tends to be as good as the selection of customers on the advisory board. Also, make sure you factor in the biases of the select few who are still your customer, still using your product, and don't want to be too critical of your product except for wanting to influence your product to meet their specific requirements. Feedback from customer advisory boards needs to be well-calibrated. Otherwise, you run into the risk of choosing a product direction that may be too over-indexed on the needs of a select few customers as opposed to most customers.

On the other hand, hiring third parties to survey your customers' needs to be carefully managed as an approach. The data third parties gather could be skewed based on the sample size of customers surveyed, customers' willingness to provide real meaty insights, and the technical depth of the third party to dive deep into the details of your product.

BE AWARE OF THREE NEW FORCES SHAPING COMPETITION IN TODAY'S WORLD

MARKETPLACES, COMMUNITIES, AND COOPETITION

To recap the words of wisdom from Michael Porter, the essence of the job of the strategist is to cope with competition. Each industry has a distinct structure that shapes the type of competition that unfolds in the industry. Porter's five forces model to analyze the operating competitive environment of a business was first published in Harvard Business Review in 1979.

Porter's five forces include three forces from 'horizontal competition.'
– the threat of substitute products or services
– the threat of established rivals
– the threat of new entrants and two others from 'vertical' competition
– the bargaining power of suppliers
– the bargaining power of customers.

Porter developed his five forces framework in reaction to the then-popular SWOT analysis, which he found both lacking in rigor and ad hoc.

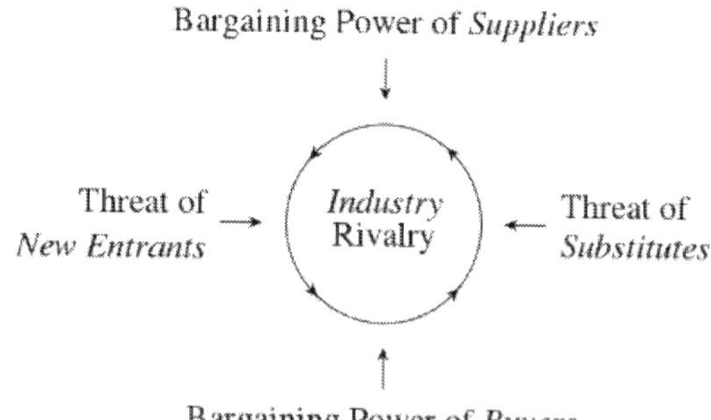

Over time, Porter's framework has been challenged by other academics and strategists. For instance, Kevin P. Coyne and Somu Subramaniam claim that three dubious assumptions underlie the five forces:

- That buyers, competitors, and suppliers are unrelated and do not interact and collude. This is particularly relevant in today's operating environment where strategic alliances are formed, and coopetition is the default way in which businesses operate. Also, this assumption falls flat when you consider doing business in countries like Japan, China, or South Korea among others.

- That the source of value is a structural advantage (creating barriers to entry).

- That uncertainty is low, allowing participants in a market to plan for and respond to changes in competitive behavior. We live in uncertain times where participants in a market do not get the luxury to plan for or wait for a response to changes in competitive behavior.

Other criticisms of Porter's five forces model are that it places too much weight on the macro-environment and doesn't assess more specific areas of the business that also impact competitiveness and profitability. Also, it does not provide any actions to help deal with high or low-force threats (e.g., what should management do if there is a high threat of substitution?).

Porter's five forces framework has since been studied in business schools and corporations to understand a business's competitive environment; however, we live in the 2020s where the operating environment for businesses has changed drastically. To site few examples:

More and more companies are shaping structures of the industries they operate in. For instance, the top few technology companies in the world like Apple, Microsoft, Amazon, and Alphabet are shaping industry structures with lines blurring between several industries.

The barriers of entry have evolved with more equal access to distribution channels and innovation in business models with the widespread adoption of internet, cloud, and AI. In general, the capital requirements to start a business have lowered significantly while late movers can now have an advantage of making more modern platform choices over early mover incumbents.

In some industries, the power of suppliers has been disrupted with regulation while in other industries the power of suppliers has multiplied.

With the threat of substitutes and intense rivalry among existing competitors and new entrants, the power of customers is at an all-time high. There are exceptions though due to the impact of recent hyper inflationary macroeconomic environment and the evolving willingness to pay due to supply shortages caused by supply chain disruptions. E.g., videoconferencing has become a viable substitute to travel, given the backdrop of the recent global pandemic. At the same time, there is intense rivalry among the likes of Zoom, Microsoft Teams, Google Meet, and

WebEx while dozens of new entrants appeared on the scene with the desire to gain market share.

Years of market-share jockeying have been compressed into months with so many workers operating from home. Millions of workers started using services from Zoom, Google, Microsoft, and Slack in no time and the world had changed rapidly. While the fundamental five forces may still exist, there are new pseudo forces that are more suitable to describe the environment businesses operate in today. E.g., ***marketplaces, communities, and coopetition.***

These new pseudo forces add new critical dimensions to the operating environment for a business. We operate in a world where all these three new forces of marketplaces, communities, and coopetition coexist and converge in unique ways underlying our relatively newer business models. Take, for example, Uber or Airbnb, both operate as marketplaces nurturing communities of drivers or travelers while establishing coopetition with their close substitutes offering more customer choice rather than feeling threatened by substitutes.

WHY INVEST IN MARKET & COMPETITIVE INTELLIGENCE?

Majority of the business leaders realize that investing in competitive intelligence is critical for most companies irrespective of the industry they operate in, especially when the industry lines are blurring across categories as companies expand into new categories or industries for growth.

Today, there is a perfect storm emerging in the form of convergence of trends:

- The amount of information readily available (44 zettabytes on the internet in 2020) to be consumed far exceeds the processing capacity of the conscious human mind (estimated at 120 bits per second or 9.88 gigabytes per day)
- Business leaders are under immense pressure to execute flawlessly during the current uncertain times of macroeconomic and geopolitical instability compounded by dynamically evolving competition, within an industry and even within the realm of global competitiveness.
- Approximately 70 percent of small businesses fail within the first 10 years and 20 percent fail within the first year (Source: Bureau of Labor Statistics, as reported by Fundera). A CBInsights analysis of 101 startups polled the reasons why those businesses failed, according to their founders.
- Even if these startups got some things right like the market fit, stable cash flow, and the right team, 19% of them still were outcompeted by another company.

This perfect storm yields the question,

"What can companies and business leaders do differently to keep up with the exponential growth in information, make sense of the world during uncertain times, and to outcompete in the industry they operate in?"

The answer lies not only in the strength of their product or brand of the company but also their ability to continuously pay attention to the evolving competitive landscape. How? **Competitive Intelligence.**

To level our understanding, let us try to understand what competitive intelligence is and why do data-driven companies build competitive intelligence flywheels.

What is Competitive Intelligence?

According to Strategic & Competitive Intelligence Professionals (SCIP), competitive intelligence is a discipline that enables organizations to reduce strategic risk and increase revenue opportunities by having a deep understanding of what has happened, what is happening, and what may happen in their operating environment.

While most companies get good at tracking what has happened with their competitors, only some can keep track of what is happening right now, and only a select few data-driven companies can accurately predict what may happen in the future. That is why the platform that can only answer what has happened in the past (like a data warehouse) may not be capable of either tracking what is happening (streaming) or predicting what will happen in the future (data science machine learning).

Market Intelligence

Rather than just talk about frameworks and concepts, let us try to dive deep into how to go about analyzing the competitive landscape your business operates in. This will offer step-by-step guidance.

- Identify top current and emerging competitors.
- Allocate time to study competitors.
- Build an internal competitive intelligence knowledge base.

Identify top current and emerging competitors!

The initial assessment starts with identifying the top 3 or 4 current competitors. By "current", we mean these competitors are actively trying to steal customers away from your business and their size/scale represents enough significance that you must pay attention to them. Though there may be new competitors emerging all the time, those may not represent as significant a threat to your business in the short term as the current competitors.

To step through an example, let us say you are Microsoft. Microsoft operates in numerous different businesses however the bulk share of the revenue comes in from three major business groups as depicted in this visual below. In each of these three business groups, Microsoft may be competing with different sets of competitors given the nature of the business and how customers choose Microsoft versus the alternatives.

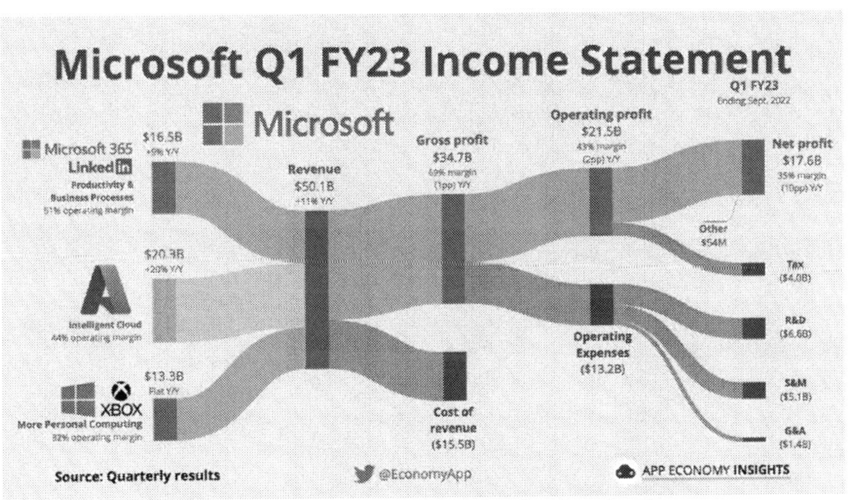

Credits: App Economy Insights for the visual.

The largest chunk of revenue comes in from Intelligent Cloud, this is where Microsoft may directly compete with the likes of AWS and GCP. On the other hand, Microsoft 365 may be competing with G Suite productivity applications or Xbox competing with Sony PlayStation or Nintendo to name a few.

Allocate time to study competitors!

Once you have identified the top 3 or 4 current competitors, it is essential that you form the discipline to study the strengths and weaknesses of each competitor. Typically, there are dedicated competitive intelligence professionals working for small to large enterprises whose primary role is to gather primary and secondary intelligence on these top competitors. In case you do not have a mature competitive intelligence function, you could also rely on third-party consulting firms who specialize in this domain and can help augment your existing capabilities to take on these competitors head-on.

The idea of studying competitors is to continuously gather and analyze intelligence related to your competitor's moves such as:

- What specific product/service capabilities of your competitor overlap with your product/service?
- What products/services is your competitor launching?
- What partnerships is your competitor announcing?
- Who is your competitor hiring?
- How did the earnings for a given quarter go for your competitor if they are a public entity?
- What specific information did your competitor share during the earnings call that they may not be willing to share as openly otherwise?
- Who did your competitor acquire?
- What specific markets is your competitor most interested in expanding into? Do such moves represent a direct threat to your core business?

A directional view of such intelligence could lead to cues on how your competitor is likely to move forward with its business strategy. Such perspective is valuable to business leaders in determining a course of action for their own businesses to help establish or carve out a specific position in the market for their business.

The open question remains: ***"how should you prioritize the top 3 current and top 3 emerging competitors if your business operates in a crowded market with dozens if not hundreds of competitors?"***

Some companies focus on competitors with either the largest revenue or largest relative market share or the largest number of customers. The objective of this prioritization exercise is to identify threats to your existing most revenue-generating product/service. You may refer to such a product/service as your flagship or core product/service.

Take, for example, Apple. Though Apple offers numerous products/services like MacBook's, iPads, smart watches, Air Pods, and app store (as depicted in the visual below); iPhone clearly can be categorized as Apple's flagship product.

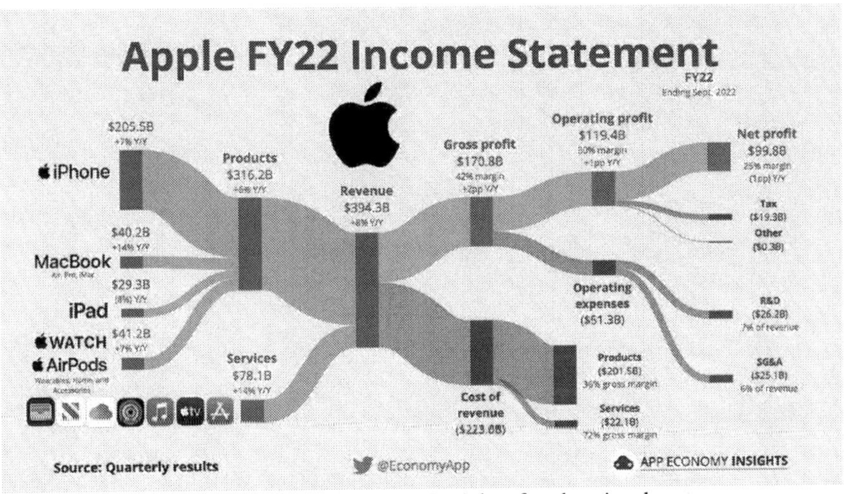

Credits: App Economy Insights for the visual.

So, how do you exactly study competitors?

Typically, you can find meaningful information about your competitors from:

- Surfing competitor's website, LinkedIn page, and job portal.
- Attending competitor's events to learn about their messaging.
- Playing with competitor's products to learn about customer experience.

Now that you have a good enough starting point for gathering competitor intelligence, what can you do with such information?

Build an internal competitive intelligence knowledge portal.

Competitive intelligence can be leveraged by several stakeholders within an organization. From the likes of C-suite to product management to product marketing managers to field sales, each of these stakeholders can benefit from the competitive intelligence you gather.

One of the best practices to scale the impact of such information is to establish a central location where different stakeholders can find such intelligence. Why is it important to establish a central location for such insights? CI functions/teams by their very nature tend to be small but mighty teams. Unless CI teams find such scaling mechanisms as establishing a central CI portal, it can eventually become very challenging for CI teams to communicate with the rest of the organization. Moreover, we live in the world of self-service consumption of information and are already overloaded with too much information arriving in our inbox each day. Such a CI portal helps separate signal from noise.

Where should you establish this CI portal?

Should this live within or integrate with existing CRM tools that your field sales use already?

It all depends on what specific stakeholders you are trying to cater to and how they prefer to consume such information within the preferred tool they already use day in and day out. Some CI teams allocate weightage to their stakeholders. E.g., 70% focus on sales, 20% on product, and 10% on C Suite. The right mix can vary based on the size of your company, how mature is your business, organizational dynamics, and what type of competitive landscape you are operating in.

If say your primary audience is sales, it would be beneficial to find ways to integrate your CI portal into the existing CRM in place or find ways to surface relevant competitive intelligence within the CRM, so sellers do not have to leave their preferred tool to find competitor-specific information. If you choose to establish a dedicated CI portal, it may be best to tier your competitors and organize information in a way that is easily consumable by your target audience.

Once such a central CI portal is in place, you could do a whole host of things like publish battle cards, measure usage metrics, and engage your target audience to seek feedback and iterate over the feedback.

If you are curious to learn about competitor intelligence, refer to an introductory course on Udemy, **"Becoming Great at Beating the Competition."**

Made in the USA
Columbia, SC
24 January 2025

52460702R10067